Traveling Together

Mary Sue Taylor

Traveling Together

PRAYERS FOR GATHERINGS

St. Anthony Messenger Press

CINCINNATI, OHIO

Nihil Obstat: Rev. Hilarion Kistner, O.F.M.
                  Rev. Edward Gratsch

Imprimi Potest: Rev. John Bok, O.F.M.
                  Provincial

Imprimatur: +James H. Garland, V.G.
              Archdiocese of Cincinnati
              May 29, 1990

Scripture selections are taken from *The New American Bible With Revised New Testament*, copyright ©1986 by the Confraternity of Christian Doctrine, Washington, D.C., and are used with permission. All rights reserved. The poem, "Journey Home," by Joy Conner, in memory of Stephen J. Deagle, is used by permission of the author. The prayer adapted from *Prayers for the Domestic Church* by Edward M. Hays, copyright ©1979, Forest of Peace Books Inc., Easton, KS 66020, is reprinted with permission. The excerpt from *Hymn of the Universe* by Pierre Teilhard de Chardin, copyright ©1961 by Editions du Seuil, is reprinted by permission of Harper & Row, Publishers, Inc. Passages from *Unencumbered by Baggage* by Carlos G. Valles, S.J., copyright ©1988 by Gujarat Sahitya Prakash, Anand, India, are used by permission of the publisher. Text from the *Revised Standard Version Bible*, copyright ©1946, 1952, 1971 by the Division of Christian Education of the National Council of Churches of Christ in the USA, is used by permission. The passage from *A Course in Miracles*, copyright ©1975, Foundation for Inner Peace, Inc., is reprinted by permission. The passage from *There Is Still Love: Five Parables of God's Love That Will Change Your Life* by Malachi Martin, copyright ©1984 by Malachi Martin, is reprinted with permission of Ballantine Books, a division of Random House, Inc.

Cover and book design by Julie Lonneman

ISBN 0-86716-120-5

©1990, Mary Sue Taylor

This book is dedicated to:

_____

(group or family)

_____

(date)

_____

_____

_____

_____

(member signatures)

Contents

Introduction

Prayer is part of a person's struggle for identity; it returns "those who pray" to their roots. The more one becomes grounded in the divine reality, the more one's actions and choices spring from the Spirit and accomplish God's will.

This book is for groups or families who want to spend "some time apart" from practical matters and worldly activity. It is the "time apart" that enables members to create a communal heart and discover what they are about. *Traveling Together* is intended for use wherever two or three are gathered in Jesus' name.

The prayers are designed for groups who meet for some purpose other than prayer—service, study, socialization, even the bonds of family relationships. Simple and comfortable, they focus on five stages of a group's common journey:

- Part One, Setting Out, addresses not only the formation of a new group, but also the smaller beginnings groups make when circumstances, projects or goals change.

- Part Two, Making Progress, offers support for the journey itself.

- Part Three is concerned with Wayside Celebrations, holidays and events both sad and joyful in the life of a group's members.

- Part Four focuses on Trouble On the Road, the internal and external storms that sometimes blow into every group's life.

- The prayers in Part Five, Traveling Alone and Together, seek the balance between individual needs and the needs of the group.

Everyone will feel at home with the prayers because they borrow structures from such familiar liturgical forms as the Prayer of the

Faithful and the Solemn Blessing at the end of Mass. They also borrow two roles from the liturgy: leader and reader.

The Roles

The role of the leader is to make the final decision on prayer selection, to be sure that a reader is assigned and prepared, to see that any needed props are in place and to lead the group in prayer.

In determining which prayers are appropriate at which times, the leader should encourage people within the group to request prayers themselves so that the leader is not always determining direction or sensing trouble. Leaders must take care that their prayer choices do not single out anyone for criticism or embarrassment. If, for instance, someone in the group is "playing for power," he or she is the one to step forward and request that prayer, not the leader.

The role of the reader is to read the selected passage *slowly* so that it has time to sink into the minds and hearts of the listeners. Some people are very uncomfortable with reading out loud, so never force this role on anyone.

Assign both roles as people volunteer for these positions. Rotate turns so that everyone who wants to serve gets a chance. The schedule of leaders and readers may be written or verbal, depending on the nature of the group and the number of people involved.

Creating a Prayerful Mood

Set a mood of reverence, quiet and attention by picking some sort of symbol, such as a candle or a chime, and using it consistently to signal prayer time. You may also want to cut the phone, dim the lights, arrange background music and so on. It's all a matter of group preference.

Let this book launch your group into communion with the divine. Then allow the Spirit to move you beyond the confines of these printed pages. And may God bless you on your spiritual journey!

2

Part One

Setting Out

Beginning

LEADER: Almighty God,
Creator of life:
you are the Alpha and the Omega
the Beginning and the End.

Together at the threshold of
a new adventure,
we stand before you
eager to begin
in accordance with your plan.

We know the way to you
because we remember your
Son's words, "I am the way, the
truth and the life," and
we understand that the
end is not a physical destination
but a state of mind.

Bring us safely to that state,
Prince of Peace,
where we can live in equilibrium
and become one with
the divine Trinity.

Father God,
give us the wisdom to know that our path is you,
to seek your way,
to proclaim your truth
and to begin a new life.
Let us end our prayer together: Glory be to the Father....

The First Step

LEADER: The Lord be with you.

ALL: And also with you.

LEADER: Lift up your hearts.

ALL: We lift them up to the Lord.

LEADER: Father, all-powerful and ever-living God, we do well always and everywhere to lift up our hearts to you.

Be with us now as we take the first steps in our new adventure.

Help us come to the knowledge that our journey is an end in itself, an end we reach only when we live each step in the present moment.

May these first few steps set the pace for our entire sojourn as we move to the beat of your rhythm, aware of and grateful that your presence constantly surrounds us.

Let us give thanks to the Lord.

ALL: It is right to give him thanks and praise.

Finding the Balance

LEADER: The response to these petitions will be "God give us wisdom."

Christ, you came as a sign of paradox to teach us the duality of our nature. Help us find balance, Lord, we pray.

ALL: *Response.*

4

LEADER: Help us walk that delicate tightrope which reconciles the visible world with the invisible, the spiritual with the material. Help us find balance, Lord, we pray.

ALL: *Response.*

LEADER: Restrain our enthusiasm when needed so that we do not hastily jump into projects without counting the cost. Help us find balance, Lord, we pray.

ALL: *Response.*

LEADER: Inflame our lukewarmness when we tend to hesitate rather than act, to withdraw rather than reach out. Help us find balance, Lord, we pray.

ALL: *Response.*

LEADER: Maker of matter, you who bring all things into balance, create in each of us a center of equilibrium so that we may steadily journey toward you. Amen.

Letting Go

LEADER: The response to these petitions is "Lord, hear our prayer."

O loving Father
Remind us that it is in letting go,
in not owning, in dispossessing
that we can travel freely.
For open hands, we pray.

ALL: *Response.*

LEADER: Merciful Master,
    free us from clinging to our friends and family so much
    that we cripple them from responding to our love.
    For open hands, we pray.

ALL: *Response.*

LEADER: Gentle God,
    help us realize that our passion to possess
    robs us of the pleasure of appreciating good things
    as they flow through our lives.
    For open hands, we pray.
    We pray to the Lord.

ALL: *Response.*

LEADER: Blessed is the God of creation, who teaches us to love
    without force or control. Amen.

Choosing a Destination

LEADER: In order to arrive at our destination, we must first know
    where we want to go in life and what we want to become.
    This is no easy decision; we are going to try an exercise to
    help us. Let's take a minute or two to think about what you
    would like people to say about you after you are dead. What
    words would you like engraved on your tombstone? If you
    could write your own epitaph, what would it be?

    Let us ask the Lord to guide our thoughts.

    Lord God, our Father
    Open us up to your will
    Help us find that special job,
    do that special task,
    become that special person you had in mind
    when you created us.

Silence (one or two minutes).

Let us join hands and say the Our Father together. After that, those who would like to may share their thoughts about how they would like to be remembered, what words or phrases they want on their tombstone.

Our Father....

At a Crossroads

LEADER: This is a blessing prayer; please respond "Amen" after each phrase.

May the all-knowing Lord,
the God of wisdom and might,
help us choose the right direction.

ALL: Amen.

LEADER: May God give us faith even when we are not sure of the way.

ALL: Amen.

LEADER: May God give us confidence when we walk in darkness and uncertainty.

ALL: Amen.

LEADER: May God's peace grow in our hearts, along with the realization that our effort to find his way is enough to please him.

ALL: Amen.

LEADER: May Almighty God bless us all,
the Father,
and the Son
and the Holy Spirit.

ALL: Amen.

Taking Responsibility

LEADER: Let us begin our prayer with this quotation from the *Course in Miracles:*

READER: I am responsible for what I see.
I choose the feeling I experience.
I decide upon the goal I would achieve.
And everything that seems to happen to me I ask for,
and receive as I have asked.

LEADER: Please answer the following petitions with the phrase,
"Lord, help us respond to our abilities."

Wise, wonderful Counselor, give us the wisdom to
understand that what we give out is what we get back, we
pray to you.

ALL: *Response.*

LEADER: Loving Creator, let us project kindness and love rather than
fear, we pray to you.

ALL: *Response.*

LEADER: Generous God, you who give us a multitude of gifts, help us
to acknowledge these gifts and share them with one
another, we pray to you.

ALL: *Response.*

LEADER: Father, you give us the freedom of choice. May we take responsibility for our own emotions and choose happiness rather than sadness, we pray to you.

ALL: *Response.*

Changing Directions

LEADER: Let us begin our prayer with a reading from Ecclesiastes.

READER: There is an appointed time for everything, and a time for every affair under the heavens.

A time to be born and a time to die; a time to plant, and a time to uproot the plant.

A time to kill and a time to heal; a time to tear down, and a time to build.

A time to weep, and a time to laugh; a time to mourn, and a time to dance.

A time to scatter stones, and a time to gather them; a time to embrace, and a time to be far from embraces.

A time to seek, and a time to lose; a time to keep, and a time to cast away.

A time to rend, and a time to sew; a time to be silent, and a time to speak.

A time to love, and a time to hate; a time of war, and a time of peace.[1]

---

[1] Ecclesiastes 3:1-8

9

LEADER: Glorious God, in your creation, there are many paths and choices. Open our eyes so that we may see all the options available.

Restrain our impulsive natures from making hasty moves.

Provide us with the patience to make slow, deliberate decisions, taking into consideration the needs of others.

Grace us with a sense of timing so that we will know when to change directions and grant us the courage to change when we sense it is time. Amen.

For Courage

LEADER: Let us begin by forming a circle, joining hands and pausing for a moment of silence to draw courage from the presence and support of one another.

Pause.

LEADER: Please respond to the following petitions with "Lord, give us courage."

God of Creation, gift us with a sense of adventure; make us unafraid to take the dangerous curves and risks necessary to live your gospel message, we pray.

ALL: *Response.*

LEADER: Christ, Love Incarnate, Lamb of God who shed your blood for us, strengthen us for the dreadful reality of unconditional love, we pray.

ALL: *Response.*

LEADER: Almighty and ever-living Father, infuse us with the knowledge and power to deal with the mental anguish involved in overcoming temptation, we pray.

ALL: *Response.*

LEADER: Lord of Light, give us the daring to be open to the blinding flash of your light instead of hiding, preferring the privacy of darkness, we pray.

ALL: *Response.*

The Path Less Traveled

LEADER: In this prayer, we hear God speaking to us. Please respond after each verse, "God, grant us the courage to try new ways."

Do not be afraid to leave the pavement where the mob moves. I will be around that unknown bend on the path less traveled.

ALL: *Response.*

LEADER: Take time away from the crowd. Even though I'm everyplace, including the heavily traveled routes, you won't notice me there because you'll have the fellowship of one another.

ALL: *Response.*

LEADER: Depart from the expressways with their well-marked signs, secure fences and smooth, graded shoulders. Give me your fears and insecurities. I will fashion you into a vessel of my own making and fill you with your own uniqueness. But I can do this only if you come to me on the path less traveled.

ALL: *Response.*

Part Two

Making Progress

For Awareness

LEADER: God of the universe,
your word and your light surround us,
but we are so often deaf and blind
to your divine presence.
Help us now to set aside our egos, our selves,
and become aware of you.
With each breath may we breathe in your love and grace.

Pause.

With each relationship,
let us affirm the good and allow the other to be.

Let us reflect for a moment on a relationship where we are
worrying and dwelling on the negatives.

Pause.

With each decision, let us choose the most loving way.

Let us reflect for a moment on a decision we are facing
where we are tempted to make a choice based on fear
rather than love.

Pause.

With each action, may we act with Christ's strength rather
than our own human weakness.

Let us pause for a silent moment to reflect on an action
where we forgot to use Christ's strength within us but
chose, instead, to cling to our own weakness.

Pause.

Help us, Father,
gently to notice those relationships, decisions and actions
where we are forgetting you.
Remind us to be aware of your grace working in our lives
so that we can act, think and choose
out of your love and strength
rather than our own fear and weakness. Amen.

For Perseverance

LEADER: O eternal One,
Wellspring of existence,
you who were there before the beginning,
you who know no end,
instill in us that wonderful quality of perseverance
which enables us
to hang on when there is nothing to grab,
to hope when all appears hopeless, and
to "believe in the sun even when it isn't shining."

Let us join hands now and together give glory to God:

ALL: Glory be to the Father,
and to the Son
and to the Holy Spirit,
as it was in the beginning,
is now,
and ever shall be. Amen.

Adjusting the Pace

LEADER: Eternal and loving God,
since time is an invention of the physical plane,
deliver us from our bondage to the clock.

Holy Spirit,
encourage us to roam freely in the faith dimension
and to let time become our guide rather than our master.

Brother Jesus,
on our journey, we will encounter fellow sojourners
moving at a variety of speeds:
from the slow steady pace of the turtle
to the quick, hurried sprint of the hare.

Creator of all good things,
let each of us, captured by the joy of dance,
move to our own unique drum beat,
all the while respecting others' right to do the same. Amen.

To the Gardener

LEADER: Sower of the seed,
may the ground of our spiritual being
be rich and soft, finely textured,
ready always for the impregnation of your seed.

Daily let us cultivate the soil of our inner space
so that it will be responsive to your divine touch.

God of rain, Water of eternal life,
refresh us with your nourishment,
cleanse us with your purifying power
and shower us with a downpour of your love.

Harden not our hearts, Lord;
remove the rocks from our barren patches
so that the stream of your Spirit will seep deep into our
souls.

Pause.

We close our prayer with a moment of quiet so that we may
get in touch with all that is hard, rocky or coarse within us
and expose it to the gardener for forgiveness.

Silence.

Amen.

For Guidance

LEADER: Please answer the following prayer petitions with the
phrase, "Lord, hear our prayer."

God and Giver of life,
We join together now to pray in unison to our guardian
    angels.
But first we give thanks to you
for providing each of us with our own spiritual benefactor.
We pray to you in gratitude.

ALL: *Response.*

LEADER: Divine protectors,
you who are the artists of our inner landscapes,
our invisible instructors, our connections to the Creator,
thank you for being there,
cheering us on along the road to the kingdom.
We pray in gratitude for your presence.

ALL: *Response.*

LEADER: Constant companions,
how often we neglect your instructions,
even forget that you are there.
Help us to remember, gentle guardians,
the power and energy that you can direct our way
to help us discover and carry out the divine will.
We pray in gratitude for your presence.

ALL: *Response.*

LEADER: Higher powers, intuitive guides,
draw together now those unseen forces
that will help us accomplish our mission and journey to
wholeness.
We pray in gratitude for your presence.

ALL: *Response.*

For a Steady Gait

LEADER: Master of the universe,
allow us to see ourselves as your children,
fully perfect, completely whole and wanting nothing.

Infuse us with the wisdom to breathe love and compassion
into everything we touch.

Let us be mindful of the words of the great poet, Pierre Teilhard de Chardin:

READER: Son of man, bathe yourself in the ocean of matter; plunge into it where it is deepest and most violent; struggle in its currents and drink of its waters. For it cradled you long ago in your preconscious existence; and it is that ocean that will raise you up to God.[2]

LEADER: Steady our gait, God, so that we do not drift off into the cloud of spiritual dreaminess, ignoring our earthly responsibilities.

Steady our gait, God, so that we may not fall into the temptations of too much matter—the temptations of flesh and creature comforts.

Steady our gait, God, so that we give glory to all of your creation.

We end our prayer with a hymn of praise:

ALL: Glory be to the Father....

Rest Stops

LEADER: All-powerful and ever-living Lord,
we do well always to remember you.

We stop for a rest now
to salute your divine presence within us,
to feel the comfort of your mercy,
the love that is unconditional,
the forgiveness that reaches infinity
and the strength that flows
from the vine to the branch.

---

[2] From *Hymn of the Universe*, by Pierre Teilhard de Chardin

You, Lord, are the Vine; we are the branches.
We rest in you.

Let us give thanks to the Lord our God.

ALL: It is right to give him thanks and praise.

Peaks and Valleys

LEADER: This is a blessing prayer, so please respond with "Amen" after each phrase.

May the God of goodness and light bless you each day with the forethought to reflect on your role and responsibility in God's majestic creation.

ALL: *Response.*

May God smile at your rejoicing as you celebrate the pleasures and successes that flow your way and grace you with the humility to ponder on the source of that flow.

ALL: *Response.*

May God console you in times of sorrow and give you the insight to learn and grow from your sufferings.

ALL: *Response.*

May almighty God bless and watch over you as you reflect on the peaks and valleys along the journey of life.

ALL: *Response.*

Prayer of Praise

LEADER: We begin our prayer of praise with Psalm 92.

READER: It is good to give thanks to the LORD,
     to sing praise to your name, Most High,
To proclaim your kindness at dawn
     and your faithfulness throughout the night,
With ten-stringed instrument and lyre,
     with melody upon the harp.
For you make me glad, O LORD, by your deeds;
     at the works of your hands I rejoice.[3]

LEADER: It is good to give thanks, and we joyfully sing your praises. For you, O Lord, have made us in your image. Awaken in us an awareness of our individual beauty and uniqueness.

How great are your works, O Lord! Open our hearts so that we may see you in all of creation and be filled with your glory, which constantly surrounds us.

Let us close by singing the Great Amen.

Sing any version which is familiar to the group. Guitar, harmonica, tambourine, chime—any of these make joyful accompaniment here.

Overcoming Obstacles

LEADER: God of creation,
     you who made the rock and the smooth places,
     the mountains and the valleys,
     help us realize that on our journey
     we will encounter many obstacles.

---

[3] Psalm 92:2-5

The wind will not always be at our backs
nor will the path be always smooth.
Give us the wisdom to understand
that what is really important is not what happens to us
but how we handle what happens to us.

Grace us, generous God,
with the ability to see obstacles as opportunities for growth
rather than causes for complaint.

Gentle God,
as you guide and direct us through the hard spots on the
    trail,
may we see crisis as a catalyst,
providing us with the chance to become stronger and more
    confident.

Eternal God,
help us make the most of what we encounter on our
    journey to you. Amen.

Detachment

LEADER: We begin with a prayer based on some thoughts of Thomas
Merton.

READER: Generous God, you who made the sun to shine on
everyone, help us to understand that a good action is never
wasted, that doing what is right is a way of being rather
than a means to an end.

Allow us to let go of the need for results and to understand
that our work may sometimes even achieve the opposite of
what we had expected.

Give us the wisdom to watch out for the signs of egoism in our service—extreme excitement at success or devastation at failure. Help us to maintain an evenness of purpose and not be disturbed by either success or failure.

Guide us then, Gentle Father, to work in peace, without forcing results, confident that all will come to fruition in the fullness of your time. Amen.

Keeping an Eye on the Road

LEADER: Keeping an eye on the road to your kingdom, Lord, we reflect on the meaning of these lines from your prayer:

READER: *(very slowly)*: For the kingdom,
the power
and the glory are yours,
now and forever.

Pause.

LEADER: To accept your authority over us, divine Master,
is to establish love as the rule of our lives
and give it the power
to reign over all our relationships and decisions.
To choose love over security, power, status,
reputation, comfort, passion, even survival,
is a difficult task.

Pause.

Imagine, Lord, if we really acted this out—
your Kingdom would be established here on earth.
Guide us along the road to you,
and help us stay focused on the riches of your Kingdom.

To close, let us join hands and slowly repeat the prayer Jesus left us.

ALL: Our Father....

Part Three

Wayside Celebrations

Welcoming Newcomers

LEADER: Lord God, we are all members of one body,
seeking to live in harmony with one another.
Grant us the gifts, generous God,
to accomplish this noble purpose
as we welcome _____ into our midst.

In our attempt to journey down the road together,
remind us often of the words of St. Paul:

READER: *(very slowly)* For as in one body we have many parts, and all the parts do not have the same function, so we, though many, are one body in Christ and individually parts of one another.[4]

Pause.

LEADER: Holy Spirit, open our hearts daily to the ever-deepening dimension of oneness.

Amen.

---

[4] Romans 12:4-5

Celebrating Accomplishment

LEADER: We are grateful, divine Provider,
that you have allowed us,
workers in your vineyard,
to reap such a rich harvest.

We celebrate this accomplishment
and acknowledge your hand in its achievement.

While we pray in gratitude for our own efforts,
we remember the wisdom of that eternal paradox:
Without effort we can do nothing
and with effort we spoil everything.

Help us Lord to get out of our own way
so that you can continue to accomplish your will
through us.

Let us close with a moment of silent thanksgiving.

Pause.

Amen.

Anniversaries

LEADER: Since this is a blessing prayer, please respond with "Amen"
after each phrase.

May almighty God bless *(group or project)* on this
celebration of its *??th* anniversary.

ALL: *Response.*

26

LEADER: May the God of creation
empower those associated with this effort
to continue to move and grow in the Spirit,
for it was in the Spirit that this endeavor was conceived.

ALL: *Response.*

LEADER: May the Lord of love fill everyone involved
with the grace to resist pettiness, jealousy and gossip
so that all may join together to serve this undertaking.

ALL: *Response.*

LEADER: May the Father of forgiveness
remind you that what matters
is not the quantity or the efficiency of your good deeds,
but the compassionate way in which you carry them out.

ALL: *Response.*

LEADER: May the eternal, almighty God bless *(group or project)* and
its continued efforts to *(purpose)*.

ALL: *Response.*

Mealtime Prayer
(Breaking Bread)

Before the meal begins, the leader holds up a roll or loaf and says:

LEADER: We come together, Lord,
not just to nourish our bodies
but also to nourish one another.

May this breaking of the bread *(break bread)*
remind us that we are "one bread, one body"
and that we may be called to break ourselves
in unexpected ways
to nourish one another and to serve you.

Let us now delight in food and fellowship. Amen.

Mealtime Prayer
(Blessing)

LEADER: As we thank the Lord for giving us this day our daily bread,
please answer "Amen" after each phrase.

May the Lord bless the earth, the sun and the rain
which produced this food that nourishes our bodies.

ALL: *Response.*

LEADER: May the Lord bless the many hands
that helped plant, grow, prepare and cook
this harvest from the land.

ALL: *Response.*

LEADER: May the Lord bless us and the food
as we break bread together,
thankful to share conversation
and a common meal.

ALL: *Response.*

LEADER: May the Lord smile on us now
as we eat and enjoy these wonderful gifts from the earth.

ALL: *Response.*

Mealtime Prayer
(Lord's Prayer)

Gather around the food or table, join hands and say the Lord's Prayer together.

Pause.

LEADER: Father, just as we pause now to acknowledge this food as
  gift from your hand,
  let us pause more and more often on our journey through
  life
  to become aware of and acknowledge your presence and
  providence
  in all persons, places and things. Amen.

Farewell
(Commendation)

Form a circle around the person who is leaving and place hands on him/her during the reading.

READER: The LORD is your guardian; the LORD is your shade;
  he is beside you at your right hand.
  The sun shall not harm you by day,
  nor the moon by night.

  The LORD will guard you from all evil;
  he will guard your life.
  The LORD will keep your coming and your going,
  both now and forever.[5]

---

[5] Psalm 121:5-8

Pause.

LEADER: May the Lord bless _____ as he (she) leaves
and keep us all united in spirit
regardless of the distances between us.

Let us together give glory to God:

ALL: Glory be to the Father....

Farewell
(Sadness in Separation)

LEADER: Almighty and merciful Creator,
the close companion you gave us for a while is going away
and we are feeling the pain of separation.

With heavy hearts, we bid _____ adieu,
for her/his absence will leave a void in our lives.

With loving hearts we wish _____ a successful journey
and take hope in the prayer that our paths will cross again
on the road to your Kingdom.

We join hands now and recite together the prayer
Jesus taught us:

ALL: Our Father....

*At the end of the Lord's Prayer, everyone offers a farewell
gesture (hug, handshake, kiss) to the person who is leaving.*

Farewell
(Blessing)

LEADER: We give thanks for _____ and the special gift she/he has been to our group. In this blessing prayer, please respond with an "Amen" after each petition.

May the Lord send you success and fulfillment
in the next leg of your journey,
and may the Lord also console us in your absence.

ALL: *Response.*

LEADER: May you leave with a happy heart, content in the knowledge that our love and prayers follow you wherever you go.

ALL: *Response.*

LEADER: And, finally,
may you be reminded that your leaving is a loss.
You shall be missed and remembered.

ALL: *Response.*

LEADER: As you go another way,
may almighty God bless and protect you:
the Father, the Son and the Holy Spirit.

ALL: *Response.*

Welcoming Back an Old Member

LEADER: Please respond, "Lord, hear our prayer."

With welcoming hearts we delight in the return of a dear friend and give thanks to the Lord.

ALL: *Response.*

LEADER: With joyful hearts, we renew our mutual affection and give thanks to the Lord.

ALL: *Response.*

LEADER: With happy hearts, we rejoice that our paths have crossed once again and give thanks to the Lord.

ALL: *Response.*

LEADER: With grateful hearts, we acknowledge the gift of this presence, and give thanks to the Lord.

ALL: *Response.*

LEADER: In appreciation of our togetherness, let us form a circle, join hands and pause for a silent moment of honor and respect for one another.

Pause.

Amen.

Thanksgiving Toast

Fill chalices, ceramic mugs, crystal wine glasses or any kind of beautiful drinking container with the beverage of your choice.

LEADER: Lord, we celebrate your original blessing
and thank you for making us in your image.

With the Psalmist, we sing your praises:

Sing joyfully to the LORD, all you lands,
 serve the LORD with gladness;
 come before him with joyful song.
Know that the LORD is God,
 he made us and his we are;
 his people, the flock he tends.
Enter his gates with thanksgiving,
 his courts with praise;
Give thanks to him; bless his name, for he is good:
 the LORD, whose kindness endures forever,
 and his faithfulness to all generations.[6]

Lord, our hearts are overflowing
with the essence of your being.

We have touched, have been in communion,
with the source of love
and now we stand as open channels
waiting for the tides of grace.

Fill our cups, Lord,
with the waters of everlasting life.

Each one lifts up filled cup.

In honor of you we now drink
as we give you thanks. Amen.

---

[6] Psalm 100:1-5

Advent

LEADER: The response to these petitions is "Lord, hear our prayer."

Come Holy Spirit,
prepare a place in our hearts for the Christ Child
so that we too may give birth to his love,
delivering it again and again into this world.
We pray in your name.

ALL: *Response.*

LEADER: Lamb of God, teach us to get in touch
with the interconnectedness of all creation,
the unity of the universe,
and be channels of your peace.
We pray in your name.

ALL: *Response.*

LEADER: Baby Jesus, may your birthday celebration
remind us of our own inner child
and inspire us with the daring
to be as vulnerable as you were.
We pray in your name.

ALL: *Response.*

LEADER: Generous God, for our Christmas present
give us the love that casts out fear
so that we may cultivate in our nature
the likeness of the Christ Child.
We pray in your name.

ALL: *Response.*

Christmas

LEADER: As we light this Christmas candle, let us reflect on John's words:

READER: The true light, which enlightens everyone, was coming into the world.
  He was in the world,
    and the world came to be through him,
    but the world did not know him.
  He came to what was his own,
    but his own people did not accept him.
  But to those who did accept him he gave power to become children of God, to those who believe in his name, who were born not by natural generation nor by human choice nor by a man's decision but of God.[7]

LEADER: Let us circle around this Christmas candle, which symbolizes the Light of the world, and pray together, responding, "Lord, hear our prayer."

  Christ Child, engulf us with your love,
  that greater agape love which allows us
  to overcome our need
  for fleeting moments of pleasure,
  we pray.

ALL: *Response.*

LEADER: Child Jesus, enlighten us with the radiance of your Way
  so we can shrug off the petty day-to-day trials,
  we pray.

ALL: *Response.*

---

[7] John 1:9-13

LEADER: Brother Jesus, you gave us the right to call you brother
when you gave us the power to recognize God as our
mutual Father.
May we reap the rewards of this rich inheritance
by recognizing you in everyone we meet,
we pray.

ALL: *Response.*

New Year

LEADER: Beginning today, Lord, let us resolve:

To experience life at its fullest
even when it brings agony rather than ecstasy,
the cross rather than the resurrection.

To say yes to each moment
by being fully present to what we are about.

To cast aside those concerns for tomorrow
which rob us of today's joys.

To acknowledge our gifts
and use them for your greater glory.

To be gentle with ourselves
as we discover our imperfections.

To be equally gentle with our neighbors, friends and
families
as we become aware of their weaknesses.

To consider our relationship with you important enough
to spend some time each day
resting in the awareness of your presence.

Let us now take a silent moment to reflect individually on
the significance of this new year.

Silence.

Amen.

Easter

LEADER: For our Easter prayer, we reflect on Paul's words to the Corinthians:

READER: Behold, I tell you a mystery. We shall not all fall asleep, but we will all be changed, in an instant, in the blink of an eye, at the last trumpet. For the trumpet will sound, the dead will be raised incorruptible, and we shall be changed. For that which is corruptible must clothe itself with incorruptibility, and that which is mortal must clothe itself with immortality. And when this which is corruptible clothes itself with incorruptibility and this which is mortal clothes itself with immortality, then the word that is written shall come about:

> "Death is swallowed up in victory.
> Where, O death, is your victory?
> Where, O death, is your sting?"[8]

LEADER: The peace of the risen Christ be with you.

ALL: And also with you.

LEADER: Lift up your hearts.

ALL: We lift them up to the Lord.

LEADER: Let us give thanks to Christ, who gives us victory over death.

---

[8] 11 Corinthians 15:51-55

ALL: It is right to give him thanks and praise.

Marriage

Pass out wine glasses to all present and fill them with champagne, wine or fruit juice. Ask the people just to hold the glasses until it is time to toast.

LEADER: As a source of inspiration to ____ and ____, who are making vows of eternal love, we share this story from the book *There Is Still Love* by Malachi Martin:

READER: Holding a glass of wine, Jesus spoke quietly to the young couple about to be married. "This," he said, "if you choose, will be the story of your love for one another." He drank some wine, and put the glass down. "You may think you know what love is." Jesus looked at [the groom] first. "And you," he turned to [the bride], "may have waited for the day when you would learn love in your husband's arms. But I tell you that love is something you will learn together. And, if you choose, and if you are true to the choice, you will drink the sweetest wine of love at the very moment when you think there is no wine left."

LEADER: As we lift up these glasses symbolizing the wine of love, we ask the Lord of love to bless the union between ____ and ____. May they cherish the wine of their love when it is sweet, when it is sour and even when the cup appears dry.

Each person touches his or her wine glass to those of the bride and groom, wishing them blessings and congratulations.

Wedding Anniversary

Husband and wife together hold a candle which will be lit at the end of the prayer.

LEADER: Holy Creator of love,
we celebrate the anniversary of _____ and _____
and their commitment to each other
and to a life of shared dreams, thoughts and feelings.

We ask your holy help
so that they may be always awake to each other's needs,
both spoken and unspoken.

May their twin pathways lead them
to the fullness of life and to you.

Protect them from the strong tides of daily troubles
that tend to pull loved ones apart.

Shield them from the social sickness of no commitment.

Show them how to rechannel the hidden streams of selfishness
that tend to separate souls, one from the other.

Lord of love, as we light this candle,
we ask that their love for each other shine as a single flame.

We pause now in prayerful silence
as the light of your grace burns into their being.

Pause.

As the flame is extinguished *(blow out candle)*, we ask God
to bless you and strengthen your hearts in love. Amen.[9]

Each person in the group may want to offer congratulations.

---

[9] Adapted from "Prayer Ceremony Renewing a Commitment Between Two Persons"
from *Prayers for the Domestic Church*, by Father Ed Hayes

Birth

LEADER: This is a blessing prayer. Please respond with "Amen" after each phrase.

Lord, you entrust us with the greatest gift of all—new life. We pray now for your grace and your blessing on this newborn baby. May you surround him (her) with love and protection as he (she) grows.

ALL: *Response.*

LEADER: May you grant him (her) the power to learn and grow from whatever suffering may befall him (her).

ALL: *Response.*

LEADER: May this newborn child grow in awareness of his (her) gifts and recognize that they are to be shared rather than guarded.

ALL: *Response.*

LEADER: Almighty Father, help us all, especially the baby's parents, to realize that this young soul is "on loan" from you. Only with your grace can we be responsible role models who reflect your unconditional love.

ALL: *Response.*

Birthday
(Light of Life)

LEADER: Let us gather together in a circle around the cake and join hands in prayer and celebration.

Lord, you came into this world to bring light to each of us
so that, through your intercession,
we too might pass on light and life.

Begin to light the candles.

As we light the candles on this cake,
we pray with grateful hearts
for the gift of life that you bestowed on _____,
and we celebrate the fact that we share this time on earth together.

Giver of life, we ask your blessing on this cake
and on the person whose birthday we celebrate.
May her (his) light grow stronger each day
and may she (he) be a beacon to others along the way,
we pray.

Sing "Happy Birthday."

Birthday
(In Gratitude for Chocolate)

Gather around the chocolate birthday cake.

LEADER: Lord and Giver of life, you who are our Father,
Help us recognize our inner child,
the vulnerable, emotionally open part of us
which is not afraid to show wonder and delight.

In the spirit of playfulness we rejoice in gleeful gratitude,
Giver of all good things,
for your gift of chocolate.
We thank you for the pleasure it brings to our palates
and the delicious flavor it gives to our dark desserts.

As we light the candles on this chocolate cake,
we ask you to bless _____ on his (her) birthday
as we sing now in childlike abandon the birthday song.

ALL: "Happy birthday to you...."

Birthday
(Blessing)

LEADER: You are an original,
created by a God of love
who wanted to share eternity with you!

We join now in this birthday blessing prayer. I ask
everyone to respond with "Amen" after each blessing
phrase.

May you, with each birthday celebration,
discover more deeply the significance of the gift of eternal
life.

ALL: *Response.*

LEADER: May your choices lead you away from a life of bondage
and toward a life in the Spirit.

ALL: *Response.*

LEADER: May you nurture the seeds of selfhood, planted in you at
birth,
so that you may harvest another of God's greatest
gifts—wholeness.

ALL: *Response.*

LEADER: May your birthday be filled with happiness and joy
and surround you with the loving care and support of
others.

ALL: *Response.*

LEADER: May God's continued blessing be upon you
as you journey closer to the Father, the Son and the Holy
Spirit.

ALL: *Response.*

Part Four

Trouble on the Road

Monotony

LEADER: Let us begin our prayer with Psalm 136:

READER: Give thanks to the LORD, for he is good,
>   for his mercy endures forever;
> Give thanks to the God of gods
>   for his mercy endures forever;
> Give thanks to the Lord of lords,
>   for his mercy endures forever.
>
> Who alone does great wonders,
>   for his mercy endures forever;
> Who made the heavens in wisdom,
>   for his mercy endures forever;
> Who spread out the earth upon the waters,
>   for his mercy endures forever;
> Who made the great lights,
>   for his mercy endures forever;
> The sun to rule over the day,
>   for his mercy endures forever;
> The moon and the stars to rule over the night,
>   for his mercy endures forever;[10]

LEADER: The response to the following petitions will be "For your mercy endures forever."

---

[10] Psalm 136:1-9

LEADER: Yahweh, help us develop the perseverance
that will enable us to keep plodding along
even when the road seems endless,
we pray to you, Yahweh.

ALL: *Response.*

LEADER: Faithful God, remind us that fidelity is finding your
presence
in the tedious tasks that we are asked to perform over and
over,
we pray to you, Yahweh.

ALL: *Response.*

LEADER: Generous God, give us the gift of living in the magic of the
moment
even when the moment seems dull and hum-drum,
we pray to you, Lord.

ALL: *Response.*

Breakdowns

LEADER: Lord, we come to you downhearted and broken.
It is hard for us to muster enough faith even to pray,
so overwhelmed are we by our problems.

Help us to remember your words, Lord.

READER: Come to me, all you who labor and are burdened, and I will
give you rest. Take my yoke upon you and learn from me,
for I am meek and humble of heart; and you will find rest
for yourselves. For my yoke is easy and my burden light.[11]

---

[11] Matthew 11:28-30

LEADER: Let us pray for insight, responding: Lord, hear our prayer.

Sometimes our burdens are too heavy
because they are ones we picked up ourselves.
Help us let go of the loads we have chosen
and lightly shoulder the burdens you bring, Lord.

ALL: *Response.*

LEADER: Free us from anxiety; renew us with your strength.
Dismiss our doubts so that we may begin our journey
anew,
encouraged by your words,
"My burden is easy, my yoke is light," Lord.

ALL: *Response.*

LEADER: Enlighten us with your will so that we will carry only your
burden
and work under only your yoke, Lord.

ALL: *Response.*

Feeling Hopeless

LEADER: Lord, we are in despair.
Gone is our joy.
Help us, for our hearts are heavy with hopelessness.
We pray to you, O Lord.

ALL: Lord, hear our prayer.

Pause.

READER: I, the Lord God, have heard your prayer
and I will bring consolation to your hearts.
Close your eyes now and get in touch with your pain.
See my light shining on the cause of your despair.
Is your life without love?
Is your favorite project faltering?
Are you suffering from dis-ease?
Is a needed ministry left with no laborers?
Are you without work?
Give me your burdens.
I will turn your efforts into love
even though the results may not be visible to you.
It is only when things appear hopeless
that true hope can be born.
Remember that you have one need only
and that need is to love.
Wherever you go, no matter what happens,
you will always have opportunities to love.
This alone is enough to fulfill you.
Feel the light of my love pouring into your pain,
burning away your burden.
Only love and peace remain.
Live on in that love.

In Fog and Uncertainty

LEADER: Lord God,
you who see all things as they truly are,
give us vision to see through the fog and uncertainty
that closes in on us now.

Pause.

The response to the following petitions will be "Lord, grant
us new sight."

For the humility to ask for help
when we cannot find our way,
we pray to the Lord.

ALL: *Response.*

LEADER: For the eyes to see God's way and God's will
in the midst of confusion,
we pray to the Lord.

ALL: *Response.*

LEADER: For the wisdom to understand what we do see,
we pray to the Lord.

ALL: *Response.*

LEADER: Lord of Light, lead us now over this foggy patch of road so
that we may stay on the path to our divine destiny. Amen.

Confusion

LEADER: God of spirit and matter,
in the midst of confusion and chaos
keep us centered in you.
When there is crisis,
help us to remain calm.
Where there is too much seriousness,
tickle our sense of humor.
Where there is weakness and destruction,
remind us of our strengths and gifts.
Give us the humility, Lord,
to see our mistakes,
since our inability to admit error
compounds the confusion.

And when everyone around us is negative,
give us the presence of mind to be positive.
You, Lord, are our source and center.
We can accomplish these things
only when we remain grounded in you.
We ask now for your help and clarity. Amen.

In the Face of Suffering

LEADER: O heavenly Father,
show us your Kingdom of love.

Inspire us to see your Kingdom
in the midst of confusion,
in the oppression of drugs and alcohol,
in the poverty of the homeless,
in the hurt of broken relationships,
in the friction between friends and lovers.

Open our eyes to the beauty of our coworkers and families.
Help us feel your presence within them.
Let our hearts speak to their hearts,
for only when we can see your Kingdom in the midst of the
world's suffering
are we able to transform our surroundings
and give life to the words:
"Thy Kingdom come,
thy will be done on earth as it is in heaven."

Pause.

Let us join hands and say the Lord's Prayer together.

ALL: Our Father who art in heaven....

For a Sick Person

LEADER: All-knowing God, Giver of life,
we ask that you restore _____ to health, harmony and
wholeness.

Painfully aware that all life is caught up in the balance of
ease and disease, we beseech you, divine Healer,
to tip the scales
and banish disease and suffering
from the body of our friend.

Invite everyone to touch the sick person.

LEADER: With these hands which reach out to touch _____,
we place him (her) in your care, Lord of health,
and we pause for a moment of prayerful silence
as your Spirit descends to provide healing graces.

Pause.

Recognizing your authority over our well-being
and trusting your divine love in all things,
we end our prayer, giving glory to you as we pray together:

ALL: Glory be to the Father....

For Someone Facing Surgery

LEADER: Brother Jesus,
You are our strength, our Redeemer;
Your love knows no bounds.
You taught us how to be free
even in adversity.

We ask you now to bless and prepare _____for surgery.
Bring the patient's mind, body and soul into harmony
so that healing and peace may be established within him
(her).

Strengthen the patient's spirit
so that fear, doubt and uncertainty drop
as he (she) places himself (herself) in your hands
and in the hands of the surgeon.

*Invite the group to lift their hands toward the person who is
having surgery in a gesture of blessing, and ask them to
respond with an "Amen" after each petition.*

LEADER: May the Lord Jesus bless and protect you as you prepare
for your surgery.

ALL: *Response.*

LEADER: At the hour of operation
may he surround both you and the surgeon
with his protection and loving care.

ALL: *Response.*

LEADER: May he grant you the grace and patience
to enjoy the free time your recuperation will allow.

ALL: *Response.*

LEADER: May Almighty God bless you
in the name of the Father,
and of the Son
and of the Holy Spirit.

ALL: *Response.*

For a Dying Person

This prayer is intended to be read in the presence of the dying person—in a hospital room, home, and so on. If this is impossible, you can call the dying friend on the phone (if she or he is capable of listening) and tell the friend that everyone is gathered at the other end and joining in this prayer—then read it. Or you can send the prayer with a card everyone has signed.

LEADER: *Read the prayer with most lights extinguished and just a candle burning. Some prayerful silence to start will help set the scene for a peace-filled goodbye.*

How wonderful is the new life you are about to begin!
Free at last from the flesh, your spirit will soar.
With you we rejoice; without you we will grieve.
Although your departure will bring you fulfillment,
it will leave us empty.
Dear friend, our hearts are breaking
as you are breaking away.
Comforted only by the knowledge
that you go into the hands of God,
do we let go.
We surround you with our love and care,
as we all pray together the following prayer:

Touching the dying person, recite together a prayer that is meaningful to the departing member: the Lord's Prayer, the words of a favorite hymn, a poem, a psalm, the rosary and so on.

Read this prayer even if the dying person is unaware or unconscious. Do not be afraid to cry or grieve in the presence of the departing person. Don't wait until the funeral to express emotion. Show the person what she or he means to you while she or he is still alive.

Death

LEADER: Oh Death, you grand and mysterious messenger,
you invite us to remember our real home and to return with
you to God.
We mourn our sister (brother), whose mortal body has
given up life,
but at the same time we celebrate with her (him),
confident that her (his) spiritual body has joined God.

Let us take a moment now to remember _____ joyfully
and to share with each other a memory or two.

Pause for a moment's silence and then begin sharing.

Lord God,
we know you have welcomed _____ into the company of
the saints,
but we feel a loss here on the physical plane.
Comfort and strengthen us, the friends and family of the
departed,
and help us deal with this separation.

Compassionate Counselor,
teach us to find solace and deal with our emptiness
by reaching out and consoling one another
through touch, tears and tenderness. Amen.

In Consolation

LEADER: My journey starts with a soft voice calling me into the
night.
I am lifted up and drawn toward a beautiful light.
I am leaving my family, friends and all other earthly things.
I am like a bird going toward the heavens, trying out my
new wings.

But as I soar upward everything becomes so clear.
Special arms are wrapped around me, removing all my
    fears.
I am a falcon, climbing high over the trees, lakes and the
    land.
A special love is gently leading me, taking me by the hand.
I have wings, I go higher and higher into the deep blue of
    the sky.
But I am leaving you and I wonder why me, Oh God, why?
I fly like an eagle or hawk but am more like a dove.
For I am leaving you all with a heartful of love.
My journey is taking me to a home far away.
That same voice promising I'll see you some day.
I leave you with so very much regret.
But please—do not grieve for me yet,
for my soul and spirit are finally free.
I go at peace into eternity.[12]

Protection From Nature's Fury

Have a candle and matches ready for this prayer.

LEADER: Protector and divine Guardian,
        shield us from the violence of the storm.
        In awe we recognize the power of the universe's
        natural forces—wind, water, fire and earth.
        In respect, we embrace and flow with the fury of these
           forces,
        aware that no matter what happens,
        we are in the safety of your bosom.

---

[12]"Journey Home," by Joy Conner, in memory of Stephen J. Deagle. This prayer was "given" to a friend of mine after the death of her brother—as if his spirit reached out to console her in her grief. Together we hope that this prayer will console others who are grieving the loss of a loved one.

May this candle we now light *(light candle)*
burn as a constant reminder of this intercessory prayer
as we pray for safety for our loved ones,
our homes and ourselves, responding "Lord, hear our
  prayer."

Father of fire,
keep us safe from flame, heat, smoke and lightning,
we pray.

ALL: *Response.*

LEADER: Holy Spirit, Ruler of the wind,
spare us from strong gales, hurricanes, tornadoes and
  cyclones,
we pray.

ALL: *Response.*

LEADER: Son of God, Brother Jesus,
you who walked on the waters and calmed the sea,
protect us from the ravages of rain and floods.
Give us your peace as shelter in the storm,
we pray.

ALL: *Response.*

LEADER: Mother Earth,
we take for granted the ground beneath our feet.
May God keep that ground firm and stable,
we pray.

ALL: *Response.*

LEADER: Loving God, we join hands around this candle for a moment
of silence to symbolize our unity and support for one
another in this time of danger.

(Silent pause of 10 to 30 seconds) Amen.

Part Five

Traveling Alone and Together

Spaces in Our Togetherness

LEADER: It is the spaces in our togetherness
that give meaning to intimacy.
O Divine Force,
you who are in perfect synchronization with all creation,
help us find a comfortable balance
between solitude and community.

Keep our touch light
so that we do not overload our relationships,
fragile craft that they are,
with the burdens of heavy expectations.

Teach us, Divine Soul,
to savor the spaces in our togetherness
as times for communion with you and with nature.
May we make use of these time-spaces
to tend to our own wounds,
so that when we return to togetherness
we each may bring to our relationships a richer self,
more nearly healed and whole,
we pray.

Amen.

Solitude

LEADER: Lord God, almighty Father,
in our solitude and vulnerability,
we stand before you.
May our hearts be receptive and our ears open
as we hear and listen to your words.

READER: But when you pray, go to your inner room, close the door,
and pray to your Father in secret. And your Father who
sees in secret will repay you.[13]

LEADER: The response to these petitions is "Lord, hear our prayer."

Father, we are aware that the road to you
leads first through our selves.
Help us to be patient with our own progress and growth,
we pray.

ALL: *Response.*

LEADER: You tell us, "Be still and know that I am God."[14]
Bless our aloneness, Lord,
as we attempt to discover you at the core of our being,
we pray.

ALL: *Response.*

LEADER: Reward us, Father, as you promised,
with the peace that comes from putting the world aside
and resting in stillness and solitude,
we pray.

ALL: *Response.*

---

[13] Matthew 6:6
[14] Psalm 46:11a, RSV

Silence

LEADER: Silence surrounds our lives
moving in and out of sound,
giving it meaning and emphasis.

It is not the noise that supports the quiet,
but the quiet that lifts up vibration,
molding its shape and tone.

May we take time to sit in silence
and view the clamor of our comings and goings,
we pray to you, Lord.

ALL: *Response*: Lord, hear our prayer.

LEADER: May we discover the healing power
of the quiet, listening approach to our problems and
anxieties,
we pray to you, Lord.

ALL: *Response.*

LEADER: As we close our prayer now with a minute of shared silence,
we ask that the quiet act as a gentle glue,
binding our group with greater harmony and cohesiveness,
we pray to you, Lord.

ALL: *Response.*

LEADER: Join hands and share the quiet for one minute. Direct your
thoughts to unity and group harmony.

Loving Ourselves

LEADER: Loving Lord, as we progress in our own inner journey, may we be reminded of the words of the retreat master, Anthony DeMello, S.J.:

READER: I used to tell you before: Change! Change for the sake of changing! So long as you don't have a strong reason not to change, change! Change is growth and change is life; so if you want to keep alive, keep on changing. Well, now I tell you, don't change. Change is impossible and even if it were possible, it is undesirable. Stay as you are. Love yourselves as you are and change, if at all possible, will take place by itself when and if it wants. Leave yourselves alone.[15]

LEADER: Heavenly Father,
may this message help us remember
that we were created in your image.
We are your masterpieces.
Help us to love ourselves as you created us,
to honor our bodies as your temples
and to stand in awe of the Spirit within.

To close, let us join hands for a moment of unified silence and salute the Holy Spirit within and among us.

Pause for a minute of silence.

Amen.

---

[15] From *Unencumbered by Baggage*, by Carlos G. Valles, S.J.

Being Alone

Divine and invisible Spirit,
we realize that many of our trials and tribulations
come because we cannot bear being alone in our rooms.

Give us the strength to stay
and cope with our own inner turmoil
rather than reach out for distractions.

Give us the peace of mind to pause
before grabbing at people, places and things
to fill the void which only you can satisfy.

Lead us, Lord, to you when we are alone on the road
so that our time apart brings us to a closer walk with you.

Amen.

Journeying Inward

Journeying inward, toward darkness,
we unmask our monsters one at a time
as we discover them in the crevices of our interiors.

Enlighten us with your grace, Lord of love,
so we can openly admit
our weaknesses and destructive inclinations.

For only when we fathom the depths
of your unconditional love and forgiveness
can we fearlessly fathom the depths of our own darkness.

Lord of light, shine on our shadows
as we journey inward, we pray.

Response: Lord, hear our prayer.

LEADER: Lord of light, let your brightness lighten our fears
not only of our own shadows but of our neighbors' as well,
so that we can courageously love even our enemies, we
pray.

ALL: *Response.*

Accepting Each Other

LEADER: Please respond to these petitions with "Lord, teach us to
accept one another as we are."

Gentle, generous God,
give us the patience to allow ourselves to unfold and bloom
each in our own time and in our own way, we pray.

ALL: *Response.*

LEADER: Help us realize that growth happens naturally in an
environment
which radiates love, acceptance and understanding, we
pray.

ALL: *Response.*

LEADER: Surround us with your grace and fill us with your love
so that we may create an environment of affirmation
here in our group, we pray.

ALL: *Response.*

LEADER: And, finally, may we grow to appreciate our diversity
rather than be overwhelmed or disturbed by our
differences, we pray.

ALL: *Response.*

Too Many Chiefs

LEADER: Lord, you have graced so many of us with the gift of leadership, grace us now with the virtue of humility so that we can serve one another.

May your words, taken from Luke's Gospel, come alive in our hearts.

READER: ...[Let] the greatest among you be as the youngest, and the leader as the servant. For who is greater: the one seated at table or the one who serves? Is it not the one seated at table? I am among you as the one who serves.[16]

Pause.

LEADER: Help us, Lord, to understand that love is not a cause,
a moment of valor or a meaningful ministry,
but a constant, daily struggle to put others first. Amen.

Playing for Power

LEADER: The temptation is strong, God,
to play for power,
to play to win,
to want things our own way.

Help us choose to work cooperatively rather than competitively,
remembering that we are, as Paul reminds us, one Body.

---

[16] Luke 22:26-27

READER: The eye cannot say to the hand, "I do not need you," nor again the head to the feet, "I do not need you." Indeed, the parts of the body that seem to be weaker are all the more necessary, and those parts of the body that we consider less honorable we surround with greater honor, and our less presentable parts are treated with greater propriety, whereas our more presentable parts do not need this. But God has so constructed the body as to give greater honor to a part that is without it, so that there may be no division in the body, but that the parts may have the same concern for one another. If [one] part suffers, all the parts suffer Cwith it; if one part is honored, all the parts share its joy.[17]

LEADER: Rejoicing, honoring and serving one another, we now end our prayer. Amen.

Openness to One Another

Ask people to join hands.

LEADER: God of Grace,
guide us in our efforts to open up to one another
in honesty and gentleness, we pray.

ALL: *Response*: Lord hear our prayer.

LEADER: Help us to unmask our many faces,
to remove the layers of pretense
and stand exposed
so that the "God in me"
may meet the "God in thee," we pray.

ALL: *Response.*

---

[17] 11 Corinthians 12:21-26

LEADER: During those times when it is difficult to reveal ourselves,
give us the presence of mind to remain silent
rather than engage in dishonest discourse, we pray.

ALL: *Response.*

With hands still joined, say the Our Father together.

Resolving Conflicts

*Pass out small pieces of paper to everyone in the group. Ask each
person to write down a conflict he or she is experiencing with a group
member, a family member and so on. Assure them that no one will see
these pieces of paper; they are going to be burned. After the papers are
filled out and folded for confidentiality, place them in a small hibachi
or other fireproof container. Place the container in the center or front
of the group and say this prayer over it:*

LEADER: Create in us a steadfast heart, O Lord,
so we can endure the hard labor
of building bridges of peace between one another.

Strike a match to the pieces of paper.

As these pieces of paper go up in ashes,
so too may our conflicts with one another burn themselves
out.

Let us take a minute of silence now to become aware of the
peace in our hearts.

Pause.

Help us, God, to seek community rather than division,
reconciliation rather than revenge,
and peace rather than conflict,
we pray.

ALL: *Response*: Lord, hear our prayer.

LEADER: Bless us, Brother Jesus,
in our efforts to discover you in each other,
we pray.

ALL: *Response.*

LEADER: Let us close by joining hands and saying the Lord's Prayer
together. Our Father....

Forgiveness

LEADER: Let us form a circle, join hands and say the Our Father
together. As we say it, become aware of the one thing that
the Father asks of us in this prayer.

ALL: Our Father....

LEADER: Our response to the following petitions will be "Forgive us
as we forgive others."

For the times we have hurt the feelings
of our brothers and sisters and crushed their dreams,
we ask for forgiveness.

ALL: *Response.*

LEADER: For the times we have hung onto our own anger and hurt
rather than allowing your divine grace to heal our wounds,
we ask for forgiveness.

ALL: *Response.*

LEADER: For our lack of faith
when we have refused to reach beyond our own humanness
and see Christ in different people and situations,
we ask for forgiveness.

ALL: *Response.*

LEADER: Almighty and merciful Father, you give us a choice in every
temptation—a chance to choose either your strength or
our own weakness. We pray in gratitude that you continue
to give us the chance to choose again. Amen.

Walking in Another's Shoes

LEADER: We begin our prayer with a quotation from Anthony
DeMello, S.J.

READER: We all carry in our heads a model of reality put there by
tradition, training, custom and prejudice. When the events
of life and the behavior of persons around us conform to
this model, we are at peace and when they don't conform,
we feel upset. Thus, what in truth upsets us is not those
persons or those events, but the model we carry with us.
This model is arbitrary and accidental. Realize that and you
will not feel upset any more at anything.[18]

Pause.

LEADER: Gentle God, each one of us has a piece of the truth,
a piece of reality like a jigsaw puzzle.
It is only when we all work together,
struggling to put the pieces into place
that we "wake up" to the whole picture.

---

[18] From *Unencumbered by Baggage*, by Carlos G. Valles, S.J.

Strengthen us in our struggle, almighty God
To see truth in another's piece of reality,
to refrain from thinking we have the answer
before the puzzle is completed,
To understand that it is only in bending
that we keep from breaking.

As your sons and daughters, God, we join hands for a
moment of silence in respect for the reality of one another.

Pause.

Amen.

Index